Bodybuilding for Boys & Young Men

Mike Mains

Copyright © 2019 by Mike Mains

All Rights Reserved. No part of this book may be reproduced or used in any form whatsoever or by any means, electronic or mechanical, or by any information storage and retrieval system, without written permission from the author. The exception being in cases of brief quotations embodied in critical articles or reviews. The information contained in this book is for information purposes only. It is intended for young and healthy individuals. The author and publisher have no responsibility nor liability whatsoever to any person or entity with respect to any loss, damage, or injury caused or alleged to be caused directly or indirectly by the information contained in this book.

Author contact: mainsmike@yahoo.com

The North Hollywood Detective Club Series

THE CASE OF THE HOLLYWOOD ART HEIST

Jeffrey Jones is a kid with a problem. A *lot* of problems. He's laughed at in school. The neighborhood bully has it out for him. And his parents treat him like a six-year-old. However, Jeffrey does have one ace up his sleeve: He's a master investigator.

When the brother of a friend is arrested for stealing a valuable painting, Jeffrey and his best friend, Pablo Reyes, form The North Hollywood Detective Club and set out to rescue him from jail. Their investigation leads them to a mysterious tattoo parlor, a glamorous television star, and a 20-year-old unsolved murder!

THE CASE OF THE DEAD MAN'S TREASURE

A treasure worth killing for. Hired by their teacher to find the driver responsible for a hit-and-run car accident, teen detectives Jeffrey Jones and Pablo Reyes stumble upon a search for an ancient treasure worth two hundred million dollars, and find themselves in a race against time with a ruthless treasure hunter who will stop at nothing to get his hands on the prize.

THE CASE OF THE CHRISTMAS COUNTERFEITERS

Two teen detectives. One criminal mastermind. And two billion dollars in counterfeit currency. What could possibly go wrong?

While the rest of the world prepares to celebrate Christmas, teen super sleuths Jeffrey Jones and Pablo Reyes uncover a plot to flood the city of Los Angeles with billions of dollars in counterfeit currency. Their investigation leads them to a master criminal, his hoodlum son, and a mysterious 15-year-old girl, who holds the key to the entire puzzle.

THE CASE OF THE DEADLY DOUBLE-CROSS

Teen detectives Jeffrey Jones and Pablo Reyes are hired by an older classmate to find her missing father. But when the man turns up dead, they're framed for his murder. On the run from the law, and with only their friends Marisol and Susie to help them, the boys engage in a frantic search to catch the real killer, before the police catch them.

Other Books by Mike Mains

MONKEY JOKES – A JOKE BOOK FOR KIDS!

Tickle your funny bone with these laugh-a-minute jokes for kids. Apes, cheetahs, gorillas, they're all here, ready to entertain you in the world's first and funniest collection of monkey jokes.

Are you ready for a gorilian laughs? Then stop monkeying around and get this book today!

Table of Contents:

Congratulations! 1
Fast, Fun, and Effective 9
Your Three Pillars of Success 11
Sleep and Rest..17
The Upper Body Squat..19
Advanced Chest and Back Training.........................31
Leg Training..33
Extreme Cases..35
The Naysayers Will Abound.....................................37
Plug Those Energy Leaks! 43
Bodybuilding as Self-Defense..................................51
Saving Your Soul – Your Ultimate Challenge.......57

Congratulations!

You are now a member of a very special group of athletes. You are now a bodybuilder.

If you're looking to build muscle fast, then this is the book for you. More specifically, if you're looking to build a deep, armor-plated chest, super wide shoulders, and thick, muscular arms in as short of time as possible, then this is absolutely the best book you could possibly own. Bar none.

We're embarking on a journey, you and I; a journey of strength, muscle, and self-improvement. I'm going to present you with an upper body exercise routine that is fast, fun, and effective. How effective, you ask? *Very* effective.

It's guaranteed to give you the utmost in bodybuilding results in the shortest time possible. Follow this routine faithfully, and you're going to see muscle growth not in months, not in weeks, but literally within days.

Stick with the program for three months and you're going to create an entirely new body.

The muscle-building routine you're going to read about in this book has never been known to fail.

Not once. Not ever.

It's turned scrawny human scarecrows into mountains of muscle. It's turned boys into men. It's done all that and more.

Let me give you a few quick examples so you'll know what to expect.

When I was 15-years-old, the strongest kid in my grade was a guy named Marshall W. He was the only guy in my sophomore class that played on the varsity football team with juniors and seniors that were 17 and 18-years-old.

Marshall was built like a moose, with a powerful chest and legs like tree trunks. He was one of the strongest guys at my school, and certainly one of the best athletes.

All of the varsity football players were on a supervised strength-training program with weights, and their maximum lifts were posted on a wall in the boys' locker room, just above the door to the coach's office.

There, in the musty-smelling locker room, you could look up and see everyone's one-rep maximum in the bench press and squat. Some of the older guys could bench 260 to 270 pounds. Marshall's best bench press was 225 pounds. That's a lot of weight for a 15-year-old to bench press.

Most adult men can't bench press 200 pounds, let alone 225 pounds. In fact, over 90% of adult men in the world today, including many who weigh over 200 pounds themselves, would get crushed under 225 pounds. Marshall weighed 180 pounds.

As for me, I wasn't on the football team, and I didn't have access to any kind of supervised strength-training program, or any program involving weights at all.

What I had was the program contained in this book.

I trained on that program for 15-20 minutes, three days a week for three full months and literally transformed my body, going from 140 pounds at a height of 5'9", to 165 pounds. That's when I decided to test myself on the weights.

One day, after my morning P.E. class, instead of rushing to change clothes like everyone else, I hurried into the weight room to see how much I could bench press.

I started with 100 pounds. The bar shot up and lowered with a clang. I was shocked at how easy it was. It literally felt like nothing. As I had never done a bench press before, balancing the weight was harder than the weight itself.

Quickly, I added 20 pounds and tried again. Same result. Another 20 pounds. Same result.

I was going to be late for my next class, but I didn't care. I wasn't leaving that weight room until I knew exactly how strong I'd become.

I kept adding weight, resting only seconds between each new attempt. When I reached 185 pounds, the weight felt heavy, but I still managed it.

The bell rang.

I was now officially late for my next class.

I went up to 205 pounds, gripped the bar tight, and completed a full range bench press. I was breathing like a steam engine, but I had to make one last attempt.

I loaded 225 pounds, got down under the bar, and pressed the weight all the way up.

Despite not training with weights at all, I was now officially as strong as Marshall W., the strongest kid in my class. I had no one to share my success with, but inside I was bursting with pride. I had accomplished something wonderful, and I had done it entirely on my own, using the exercise routine you're going to read about in this book.

Here's a second example I'd like to share with you, concerning just how effective this muscle-building program is. It involves a friend of mine and his twin brother.

As teenagers they both got hooked on the muscle bug and decided to improve their bodies.

What was interesting was that they each followed a different path. One brother went on a standard bodybuilding program using weights. His exercises consisted of barbell curls, squats, military presses and bench presses (a lot of bench presses), along with some dumbbell work. His twin brother followed a routine like the one in this book.

After three months, who do you think made faster and more noticeable progress? Yup, you guessed it, the twin who followed the program in this book. In fact, the difference was striking.

The brother who followed the standard bodybuilding program with weights looked better than he had three months ago. He was more muscular and certainly in better shape.

But his twin brother, the one who followed a routine like the one in this book, literally transformed himself. He looked like a mini-Hercules after only three months.

A third and final example to demonstrate the effectiveness of the routine in this book occurred to me while I was in Marine Corps boot camp. (Note: I do NOT recommend anyone joining the United States military under any circumstances. The police force, maybe, but the military, no. If you're considering joining the military, email me first and I'll tell you why I don't recommend it.)

I was 18-years-old then and built like a Roman gladiator, with muscles everywhere. About a third of the way through 12 weeks of boot camp, the platoon's senior drill instructor shouted my name.

In boot camp, when a drill instructor yells out your name, you have to drop everything you are doing and run to him as fast as you can.

Meanwhile, everyone else in the platoon has to stop what they are doing and shout out, "Sir, Private Mains! Aye-aye, sir!"

So I ran to his office, and as I stepped inside and stood at attention, the verbal onslaught began.

If you've ever heard a Marine Corps drill instructor shout, then you know what I'm talking about. He cursed and screamed and used language that I have never heard before or since.

And the more he yelled, the angrier he became. This went on for several minutes, his voice echoing through the entire barracks.

At one point, he overturned his metal desk and sent it flying across the room, where it thudded against the wall and then clanged to the floor, drawers spilling out and papers flying everywhere.

The source of his anger was the physical condition of five of the privates in our platoon. Three of them were 119-pound weaklings, unable to do more than three or four shaky push-ups. Two others were grotesquely overweight and unable to perform a single pull-up or sit-up.

The Marine Corps has strict physical requirements and if these recruits were unable to pass the required physical tests, they would have to repeat the 12-week basic training program until they could.

No matter how long it took.

Even if it took years.

"Mains!" the senior drill instructor shouted at me, his face beet red and the veins on his neck quivering, "I'm making those privates your responsibility. If those privates fail, you fail. If one of those privates has to repeat 12 weeks of boot camp, you're going to repeat it right along with him." And on and on it went while my mind raced, wondering how in the world I was going to pull this off.

The senior drill instructor was no fool. He had singled me out, because of my physique, figuring that if anyone could get those privates in shape, it was me.

And now he had just made his responsibility my responsibility.

"Do you understand?" he screamed.

"Yes, sir!"

"Then get the **** out of here!"

I got out as quickly as I could.

As my mind cleared, I realized that I was faced with a real challenge. The two obese privates each weighed over 260 pounds. They would have to lose a combined 120 pounds, minimum.

The three underweight privates looked like human skeletons. They would have to gain a combined 120 pounds, minimum, while simultaneously increasing their strength levels.

In boot camp you had exactly one hour each evening of free time to shower, write letters, or do whatever. That was it. The rest of the day was filled with military training.

From this point on, I would have to spend a portion of my free time each night training those privates so they could pass their physical tests. It would leave me with virtually no time for myself at all.

What's more, I would also have to supervise what those men ate, which meant double rations for the skinny privates and no pastries or starches for the overweight ones.

In boot camp, you only have six or seven minutes to eat a meal. That's it. For that reason, skinny privates went to the front of the line, so they could eat as much as possible in the few minutes allowed, while overweight privates went to the end of the line. They would be forced by time to eat as little as possible. You can only gobble so much food in four or five minutes.

Since I was now personally responsible for the overweight privates, I would have to fall back to the end of the chow line at every meal to make sure they weren't sneaking pastries onto their tray, which they sometimes attempted to do.

That meant less time for me to eat. I would have to eat each of my meals in five minutes, max.

I also had to choose my own food wisely in order to set an example for the others.

I couldn't tell the overweight privates not to eat pastries or starches, while I loaded up on them myself. And there were occasional moments when I craved a baked potato, a portion of pasta, or a slice of toast or pizza.

The same with liquids; soda and soft drinks were out. Milk or just plain water was in.

In a way, this was the ultimate challenge. The physical training protocol of the Marine Corps, which had worked successfully for over 100 years, had failed these five privates. Could I succeed with my own personalized training program?

By now, you should know the answer.

Yes, I did succeed.

And the change in these young men was startling.

The skinny privates each gained from twenty to thirty pounds of muscle and increased their strength tremendously.

The two overweight privates each lost forty pounds and looked like musclemen.

One of the obese privates had been unable to pull himself higher than six inches on the pull-up bar when we started. After two months of training on the system in this book, he performed 8 complete repetitions on his final test.

I'll never forget the look of astonishment on his face when he dropped down from the bar and turned to me. "I got eight!" he said.

I don't know who was prouder, him or me.

Once again, the routine outlined in this book worked.

It worked for them.

It's worked for countless others.

It will work for you too.

Shall we get started?

Fast, Fun, and Effective!

The exercise routine we're going to follow is based on the three "F"s: Fast, Fun, and Effective. It's also safe, which is a fourth "F".

It's fast in two ways. First, in the sense that it will only take you around 15-20 minutes to perform, three days a week. And second, in how quickly you are going to see results.

If you want to stretch your muscles before you start, and/or workout at a more leisurely pace, that's fine. In that case, it will take you around 30 minutes to perform.

Don't think that by training longer you'll make better progress. Your muscles grow when they are resting, not when they are being used.

That's a hard concept for many people to grasp, but it makes perfect sense when you think about it. First you stimulate your muscles with exercise, and then they grow while you sleep and rest.

The exercise routine you're going to follow is also fun. There's no pain involved, only the thrill of physical exertion. You can do these exercises alone in your room, in your basement, wherever.

Nobody has to see you. They're totally safe.

Some people like to listen to music when they train, others like silence. You can try both ways and see what works best for you.

One thing you'll notice is your muscles pumping up. That happens when blood fills the muscle and causes it to swell. It's actually a pleasurable feeling, one that you'll get hooked on.

Finally, our routine is effective, as you've already learned. It's going to work for you and transform your body in ways you've never dreamed of. So buckle up and enjoy the ride.

Your Three Pillars of Success

Think of your exercise program as a tripod, or three-legged stool. If all three legs are strong, then so is your tripod or stool. But if one leg is weak, even just a little, then the whole thing tips over and crashes to the floor.

The three legs of your program are 1) Nutrition 2) Rest 3) Exercise. In order to succeed, you'll need all three legs to remain strong and sturdy.

We're going to start with the first leg: nutrition.

I know most of you are eager to jump right to the exercises, but remember – all three legs of your program are important. If I start with the exercises first, some of you won't bother to read the information on nutrition and rest, which will slow your progress.

The first leg of your tripod, nutrition, can be a little confusing, so I'll try to simplify it as much as possible. Basically, your muscles need nourishment in order to grow, and the basic building block of muscle tissue is protein.

Your best protein sources are wild, ocean-caught fish, such as wild salmon (not farm raised) or wild mackerel; beef and liver from grass-fed animals (not grain fed); fertile eggs from pastured chickens (not caged chickens); and raw milk from grass-fed cows. (Note: Raw milk is only available in a handful of states. If yours isn't one of them, then I would avoid milk completely.)

If you're reading this and going, "Huh?" don't freak out. A little reading on the subject will get you caught up quickly.

And don't neglect eating liver, because you don't like the taste. Beef liver from grass-fed animals is nature's multi-vitamin; the most nutritious food on the planet. Raw liver (frozen for at least two weeks) from clean sources can restore energy and vitality to even the most exhausted organism.

In addition to protein, you want to consume organic fruits and vegetables. Fruits are best eaten alone in snacks. Vegetables, particularly green vegetables, such as broccoli, lettuce, asparagus, etc., can be eaten with your protein. (Protein, starches, and fruits require different enzymes in order to digest properly. For that reason, starches and fruits should always be eaten separately and not at the same time as other foods.)

Vegetables can also be juiced. It takes a while to get used to the taste of raw celery juice, raw cucumber juice, or raw carrot juice, but those juices are loaded with nutrients.

Ideally, you want to consume three to four meals a day, each one consisting of one protein source and at least one vegetable. You can include a fruit snack between meals if you get hungry. Ripe bananas (yellow with a few small brown spots on them) are great for snacks. Just be sure to eat them alone, at least four hours after a meal, or one hour before a meal.

If you have access to raw milk, drink it alone about an hour before meals. Don't drink it with your meals. In fact, don't drink any liquid with your meals. Instead, consume liquids an hour before eating. This is especially important if you are overweight.

Chew slowly when you eat and take your time. Make your meals as pleasurable as possible. With each mouthful of food you consume, think about how that food is going to fuel your muscles and make them grow.

Foods to avoid are anything that contains sugar, as well as anything that comes in a bottle, jar, bag, wrapper, or can. Basically anything that's processed or is not organically grown. Don't eat soy or synthetic meat alternatives. Avoid all fast food.

When you buy produce, look at the little numbered sticker. If you see a 5-digit number, beginning with the number 9, then the produce is organic. That's what you want.

If you see a 4-digit number, beginning with the number 4, then the produce is conventional, which means it was grown with pesticides. That's what you don't want. But if you're stuck, you're stuck. Conventional produce with peels, like bananas and oranges, are not as bad as produce without peels, like apples and grapes. I eat conventional Dole bananas on occasion, as well as conventional broccoli that's well rinsed. But they're never my first choice.

If you see a 5-digit number, beginning with the number 8, then the produce is Genetically Modified. That's what you absolutely do not want, under any circumstances.

I realize that eating for muscles and health is a tall order, so do the best you can. Don't stress out if you have to consume conventional (non-organic) produce from time to time, or if you decide to eat in a restaurant, or if you're stuck eating the junk they feed you in school; just do the best you can.

You might have to do a little searching and/or have your parents do a little searching in order to locate wild, ocean-caught fish; beef and liver from grass fed animals; and organic produce. But it's well worth the effort. You'll feel healthier, look better, and think clearer. Plus, you'll be providing your muscles plenty of fuel to grow on.

Needless to say, you want to avoid all alcohol, cigarettes, and drugs.

If you are underweight and looking to increase the size of your muscles, you're simply going to have to eat more. That doesn't mean stuffing yourself; it means a gradual increase in both the frequency of your meals, as well as the quantity of food you eat.

If you're currently eating twice a day, increase that to four times a day. If you're eating three times a day, increase that to five times a day. Slowly increase the amount of food you eat. If you eat two eggs and one slice of toast every day for breakfast, increase that to three eggs and two slices of toast every day for one or two weeks. Then increase to four eggs and two slices of toast, and then to five eggs and three slices of toast, etc.

If you are overweight, do the opposite. Cut down on the amount of food you eat, as well as the frequency. However, don't eat less than three times a day. Your muscles need fuel to grow.

Proper nutrition is vital to your bodybuilding progress, so don't neglect it.

Trying to grow muscles on a diet of sugar, soda, candy, cakes, pastries, cereal, white bread, ice cream, fast food hamburgers, French fries, and all-around junk is a daunting task. I'm not saying it's impossible, but it is extremely difficult. Why put yourself behind the eight ball when you're just starting out?

If you really want to study up on nutrition, there's a marvelous book called *Nutrition and Physical Degeneration* by Dr. Weston Price. It might be available at your local library.

Dr. Price was a dentist who traveled around the world in the 1930s, studying the teeth and general health of indigenous people (people native to a land). What he found was startling: indigenous people, eating a natural diet with no processed food whatsoever, had excellent dental health and strong, physically fit bodies.

They had no cancer, no heart disease. Many of their communities had no form of police department or jail, because there was no need for them. However, when they began eating processed food, imported by explorers and settlers, everything changed.

Their health deteriorated rapidly. Crime and delinquency became problems. Cancer, heart disease, and other illnesses that had been nonexistent before, suddenly appeared. The same food that most Americans consume on a daily basis destroyed these people. Don't let it do the same to you.

If you want perfect teeth and the strongest, most muscular body possible, then one of the best pieces of advice I can give you is to read Dr. Price's book and follow his diet recommendations. There's only one problem. The book is extremely long and makes for some pretty stiff reading.

A far more efficient way to absorb Dr. Price's research is to go online, search for his name, and visit the various websites dedicated to him, such as www.price-pottenger.org or www.westonaprice.org.

Of course, the absolute best way to learn about Dr. Price and his work is to read the book *Cure Tooth Decay* by Ramiel Nagel, available on the internet. It's an excellent summary of Dr. Price's work and it's very easy to read.

If your parents are giving you a hard time about the kind of food you want to eat, give them a copy of *Cure Tooth Decay,* so they can study the research themselves. As I write this, the book is currently selling for around $20.

Nutrition is the first leg on your tripod of success. Rest is the second leg.

Sleep and Rest

Your muscles need rest in order to grow, so do your best to sleep from eight to ten hours a night. If that's not possible, then try to get at least seven hours of sleep. Less than that is pushing it. It's possible to get by on less than six or seven hours of sleep a night. I've done it for long periods, but I don't recommend it, especially for a teen.

You'll find it easier to enjoy restful sleep if you make your bedroom as quiet and as comfortable as possible (100% cotton sheets and bed clothes will help).

If you have trouble falling asleep, try eliminating all sound, starting around thirty minutes before you go to bed. By that, I mean no talking, no music, no television, no sound at all. Your mind will quiet down considerably and you'll find it easy to nod off and enjoy a restful night's sleep.

In addition to sleep, practice resting throughout the day. If you're trying to pack muscle on your body, then you can't be running around all day, involved in all different kinds of sports and activities. You can certainly participate in sports, such as baseball, basketball, football, wrestling, etc., but don't overdo it.

Also, I wouldn't recommend long distance running. Running one mile, two miles, maybe even five miles is okay. But people who run marathons tend to be extremely skinny and weak.

Now for a big one: emotional stress.

It's really hard to gain muscle when you're under emotional stress. It can be done, as you saw earlier in my boot camp story, but it's not easy.

Plus, in boot camp, where you're being yelled at and told how worthless you are every minute of every day, after a while you become used to it. At that point, it becomes more a case of extreme physical and mental stress, rather than emotional stress. The kind of emotional stress I'm talking about is dealing with parents, school and government bureaucracy, friends (so-called), and girls.

We'll discuss each of those a little later in this book. In the meantime, practice calming your mind. Maintain poise at all times. Never let your emotions get the better of you, and don't allow your emotions to dictate your actions.

Letting your emotions get the better of you, and letting your emotions dictate your actions are both signs of weakness. Women behave that way. So do soy-boys. Don't be like them.

That takes care of the first two legs of your tripod of health and strength. The third leg – the one you've been waiting for - is exercise.

The Upper Body Squat

Are you ready for some muscle?

First, a few quick pointers: train three days a week, with a day of rest in between workouts. As we discussed earlier, your muscles grow when they are resting, not when they're being used.

Wear loose clothing when you train. If you're exercising at home, it's best to do it barefoot.

Don't hold your breath when exercising. Continue to breathe, exhaling at the point of exertion: when you are pushing or pulling against resistance, and inhaling when you are lowering the resistance.

When you perform an exercise, it's called a repetition, and a group of repetitions is called a set. Thus, if you performed an exercise five times, that would be called five repetitions - or five reps, for short - for one set. It would be written as 1 x 5.

If you did five reps, rested a minute or two, and then did another five reps, it would be called two sets of five reps, and it would be written as 2 x 5.

As I mentioned earlier, when I first performed this program, I was 15-years-old, and weighed 140 pounds at a height of 5'9".

Three months later, I weighed 165 pounds with shoulders so wide the people around me were shocked.

Your results might be similar, or they might be greater than mine. Whether in bodybuilding, or any other area of life, don't compare yourself with others. You're in competition with yourself. So strive to better yourself, and leave others alone to do the same.

Your exercise routine will contain two primary exercises: Jackknife Pushups and Chin-Ups, along with some flexing and tension exercises.

If you don't have access to a chin-up bar, don't worry. You can either skip the exercise or find a way to improvise.

Most schools have a chin-up bar somewhere on the premises. If you can sneak off and do a set or two while no one is around, great. You can also rig up a bar at home. In my case, I found an eight foot metal bar that someone was throwing away next to a dumpster.

I took it home and found a place in my kitchen where I could lay one end of the bar across a shelf in one of the cabinets, and then lay the other end across a shelf in another cabinet about six feet away.

It was slightly uneven, so I put some magazines under the low end until the bar was level. Since then, I've a chin-up bar.

Once you start bodybuilding, you'll find that can improvise just about any exercise.

The first exercise in your routine is the Jackknife Pushup. This exercise is so effective and so result-producing that I call it the upper body squat.

Bodybuilders who train with weights consider squats performed with a barbell across the upper back to be the most result-producing of all exercises. In fact, barbell squats have such a successful history when it comes to building muscle they've achieved almost legendary status. Those who promote barbell squats are right in one sense. Barbell squats are an effective exercise when it comes to building muscle, however, they also produce tremendous compression on the spine, and for that reason I do *not* recommend them.

In fact, I would make the argument that spinal compression produced by barbell squats will prevent a person from growing to their full height. In other words, they will stunt your growth. And that's the last thing you want.

Jackknife Pushups will do for your upper body – specifically for your shoulders – what barbell squats do for the lower body and back, only in total safety and without compressing your spine.

I consider Jackknife Pushups to be the King of upper body exercises. They're certainly the king of upper body exercises when it comes to thickening and broadening your shoulders. Your shoulders are going to grow so wide from doing this exercise, that your family and friends will literally be shocked. Guys will notice. And so will girls.

To perform a Jackknife Pushup properly, assume a position similar to a pushup, only with your bottom high in the air. In other words, your feet will be close together and touching; your hands will be flat on the floor, a little wider than shoulder width apart; and your hips will be pointed up towards the ceiling. With your eyes focused on your feet, you may feel like you're upside down.

From this position, bend your arms and slowly lower your head to the floor. Touch your head lightly to the floor (don't bang your head) and then press back up. You should feel this exercise in your shoulders. The average person will be able to do around eight repetitions of this exercise. For your first workout, do five or six repetitions.

Immediately after finishing your set, lower yourself to your knees, and while kneeling on the floor, extend your hands to your sides, elbows bent and palms up.

Pretend you have a heavy log resting on the palms of your hands and strive to push it up, only don't move your hands. Imagine you are pushing against the log and feel the tension in your shoulders. Do this for several seconds. This is a great tension exercise for the shoulders.

Every time you finish a set of Jackknife Pushups, do several seconds of this tension exercise. Between these two exercises, your shoulders are going to pump full of blood.

Once you get the hang of doing Jackknife Pushups, you can experiment with your hand position, moving your hands a little closer together, or a little further apart. Do what feels best for you and what produces the best feeling (best pump) in your shoulders.

You can also experiment with the way you lower your head to the floor. You can try touching your forehead to the floor, or touching the top of your head. Touching your forehead is a little easier, but touching the top of your head puts more tension on the shoulders. Again, use what works best for you.

Do the same with the tension exercise: experiment with different hand widths.

For your first workout, do a set of five or six reps of Jackknife Pushups, rest a minute or two, and then do a second set. And follow each set with the tension exercise for your shoulders.

If five reps are too many for you, then just do one or two.

If you can't do any reps at all, just hold the top position for as long as you can and/or try lowering yourself a couple of inches at a time until you are able to complete a full rep.

Remember, you're competing with yourself, not anyone else. So don't feel bad if you struggle at first. Your progress will come very fast.

For your first week, do two sets of Jackknife Pushups, followed by the tension exercise. Rest a minute or two between sets.

For your second week, do three sets with a minute or two of rest between each one.

For your fourth week, do four sets.

Four sets will be your max.

Try to add a rep or even a couple of reps each workout until you are doing four sets of twenty repetitions. By then, if you've eaten enough nutritious food and gotten enough sleep and rest, your shoulders will be anywhere from one to three inches wider than they are now. That's a lot of muscle growth.

Once you are doing four sets of twenty repetitions, stay at that level for a couple of weeks, and then begin making the exercise progressively harder by doing your last set with your feet on a small stool or chair, around 12-15 inches high.

That angle will make the exercise much more difficult as you will now be lowering more bodyweight than before. You will probably have to start that last set at five reps and then build up again. You may also need to start resting three or four minutes between sets.

When you are able to do fifteen to twenty repetitions on your last set with your feet raised, start doing your second to last set the same way.

When you are able to do fifteen to twenty repetitions on your last two sets with your feet raised, start doing your second set the same way.

Eventually, you will reach the point where you are doing one set the normal way, with your feet on the floor, for twenty repetitions; followed by three sets of fifteen to twenty repetitions with your feet raised. And you will be doing several seconds of the tension exercise after each set of Jackknife Pushups. At this point, your shoulders are going to be extremely wide.

Stay at this level for a few weeks, and then increase the progression by doing your last set with your feet on a slightly higher surface, and then work your way up as before.

Every now and then, you can do all four sets with your feet on the floor for a light workout. It's good for the body to mix things up. An occasional light workout is not a bad idea.

It's also not a bad idea to take a full week off every three or four months. The rest will do your body good.

So that's your core upper body exercise: the Jackknife Pushup. The second exercise in your program is Chin-Ups.

Chin-Ups are pretty self-explanatory. You grip the bar and pull yourself up until your chin clears the bar. Then you lower yourself down; all the way up and *almost* all of the way down. Stop just before you reach full extension at the bottom and then pull up again.

Grip the bar with your *palms facing you*, hands about shoulder width apart. Feel your biceps bulge and contract at the top of the movement when your chin clears the bar. Chin-Ups done in this manner will build your biceps like no other exercise, even better than barbell curls.

Perform two sets. Similar to Jackknife Pushups, you can experiment with different hand widths. I do my first set with my hands around shoulder width apart, and my second set with my hands around nine to ten inches apart.

When you do Chin-Ups, look up at the ceiling, not straight ahead, and think of pulling your elbows down and back.

It's okay to swing your legs out in front of you as you pull up. Doing so will allow you to pull yourself higher.

After each set of Chin-Ups, you're going to do a flexing exercise for your biceps. Hold your right arm out to the side of your head, as if you were going to make a muscle. You've seen plenty of athletes and musclemen do this when they flex their biceps. Do the same thing only don't clench your fist. Instead, keep your hand open and twist your thumb back and up.

You should feel a bulge in your bicep. Hold this for a few seconds and then clench your fist and flex your bicep conventionally.

Do the same for your left arm.

If you have trouble feeling this exercise, try touching your ear with your little finger and then turning your thumb back and up. Again, you should feel a contraction in your bicep. You can also try doing this with your hand behind your head.

You want to feel the bicep muscle contract, bulge, and flex, and then try to expand or bulge it out even more.

Chin-Ups with your palms facing you, followed by the flexing exercise will build your biceps very rapidly. Start with two sets of one or two reps in Chin-Ups and build up from there. When you can do two sets of six reps, you are really getting somewhere. At that point, you can begin doing three sets.

If you can't perform a single rep, try hanging from the bar for increasing lengths of time, along with pulling yourself up an inch or two. Gradually increase the height you are able to pull until you can do a full rep. It might take a few weeks. It might take months. But eventually, you'll get there.

If you want to build your forearms, add an additional set or two, only do them with your *palms facing away from you* and your hands around three or four inches apart. Chin-Ups done that way will really build your forearms.

You can build forearms as big and as muscular as Popeye's with a couple of sets done that way.

If you don't have access to a chin-up bar at home, but you do have one at your school or place of employment, then it's okay to do your Chin-Ups on their own for a couple of minutes, and then do your Jackknife Pushups at a different time when you are home. You don't have to do the two exercises at the same time, or even on the same day.

Now if you don't have access to a chin-up bar at all, and you are unable to improvise an alternative, just do the flexing exercise for your biceps. You can build great size in your biceps with that exercise alone.

For the rest of your body, we are going to do flexing and tension exercises. You can do these exercises every day as they are extremely easy to recover from.

Don't hold your breath when doing these exercises, or when doing any exercise. Always continue to breathe.

For your triceps (the muscle on the back of your arm), hold your arm at your side, and then consciously straighten your triceps by pulling the muscle up. At the same time, raise your shoulder towards your ear. You should feel the muscle on the back of your arm tighten and contract. Hold that feeling for about six seconds, and then do the same with your other arm.

For your chest (pectoral muscle), stand naturally, and then bring your shoulders and arms down and in. Your pectoral muscles will bulge and flex. You can do one side at a time, if you want, or you can do both pecs at the same time. Hold for six seconds.

You can also bend forward at your waist and push down towards the floor with your hands, while contracting your pectoral muscles. Or stand upright and expand your chest outward, trying to bulge your pectoral muscles out as far as possible.

For your stomach, bend forward slightly and blow all the air out of your lungs. Then pull your belly button in until it touches your backbone. Obviously, you won't be able to do that, but that's the feeling you want. Hold for about six seconds.

This exercise is called a Stomach Vacuum. It won't build your abdominal (stomach) muscles, but it will shrink your waist. Perform this exercise every day after you wake up, and also just before every meal. No one needs to know you are doing it.

To build abdominal muscle, take a breath and then exhale slowly while flexing and tensing your stomach muscles.

For your calf muscle, place one leg slightly in front of the other and then rise up on your toes. You will feel your calf muscle contract tightly. Hold for six seconds and try to push that calf muscle out as far as it will go. Do the same with your other leg.

For your thighs, slide your right leg a foot or two behind you, toes pointed, and contract the muscles on the front of your right leg and the right side of your butt. You should feel both very strongly. Flex those muscles hard for six seconds, and then do the same with your left leg.

Stand with your feet comfortably apart, as if you were going to press a heavy weight overhead, and flex your thigh and butt muscles. Hold for six seconds. To better feel this exercise, you can even raise your arms overhead, as if you really were pressing a heavy weight.

Place one leg at a time to the side, toes pointed sideways, and flex your thigh muscle.

For your hamstrings (the muscles on the back of your leg), stand normally, and then curl your right leg up behind you. You should feel a contraction in your hamstring. Go easy at first, as the hamstring muscle is easily pulled. As you gain strength, increase the intensity of your contraction and hold it strongly for six seconds. Do both legs.

With your hamstrings, you might find better leverage and a better feel in your muscles if you lean forward while curling your leg. Experiment and find what works best for you.

That completes your exercise routine.

Do your Jackknife Pushups and Chin-Ups three days a week, with a day of rest between workouts. Do your flexing and tensing exercises every day. They only take a few minutes.

Breathe during all of your exercises. Exhale while exerting. With your Jackknife Pushups, breathe in as you lower your body and breathe out as you push your body up. When flexing, breathe out as you contract the muscle.

You want to finish your workouts feeling pumped, refreshed, and energized, not worn out. If you push yourself to the point where your muscles are quivering and shaking, it's going to be very hard for them to recover. In fact, recovery from such a workout can take weeks. Most weight trainers push themselves to that point and end up in a state of chronic overtraining. As a result, they don't make any gains. Eventually, they quit training.

Train hard, yes. But don't overtrain.

The old-timers coined a saying for this: Train, don't strain.

Remember to get plenty of sleep and rest.

Remember to eat good, nutritious food, and try ingesting some protein within twenty minutes after finishing your workout. This can be as simple as a glass of raw milk, or it can be a complete meal.

The body thrives on regularity, so try to train around the same time every day. You don't *have* to do this, but it's beneficial if you can.

Along with regularity in your training, try to eat at the same time each day. And try going to bed at night, and rising in the morning at the same time every day. Your body is going to love you.

Linebacker Von Miller of the Denver Broncos understands this. He wanted to gain eight pounds of muscle over the 2019 offseason, so he spent more time in Denver over the spring and summer – something he hadn't done in the past - in order to follow a regular workout schedule. He knew from experience that regularity in all aspects of training – exercise, nutrition, and rest – is conducive to big gains.

If your current situation does not allow regularity, then do the best you can. You can build muscle on all kinds of wacky schedules. It's not easy, but it can be done. And if others have done it, why not you?

Above all, think positively.
Dedicate yourself to success.

Advanced Chest and Back Training

After completing three to four months of Jackknife Pushups and Chin-Ups, your shoulders and arms should both be considerably bigger. You can continue the program just the way it is for another three to four months, or you can do some advanced training for your chest and back.

Switching from an emphasis on your shoulders and arms to an emphasis on your chest and back is easy. All it requires is two simple changes.

First, switch from doing Jackknife Pushups to doing regular Pushups on the floor. This will focus the exercise on your chest muscles, and to a lesser degree on your triceps.

Second, switch from doing Chin-Ups with your palms facing you to doing Pull-Ups with your palms facing away from you and your hands wider than shoulder width apart.

This change in grip will focus the exercise on your latissimus dorsi muscles. The latissimus dorsi - or lats, for short - is the wide sweeping muscle that extends from under your armpit to your waist.

Nothing builds this muscle faster than Pull-Ups performed with a wide overhand grip.

Starting with Pushups, perform them in the same manner as your Jackknife Pushups, with two sets of five to six reps, and then slowly build up to four sets of twenty reps.

Use perfect form with your feet together, your back straight, and your eyes looking straight ahead, not down. Tense your entire body, lower yourself all the way down until your lower chest touches the floor, and then press back up. The only thing that should move is your arms. Follow each set of Pushups with six seconds of flexing exercises for your chest.

When you are able to do four sets of twenty reps in the regular floor Pushup, you can increase the resistance by placing your feet on a small stool or chair for your last set. Start with five or six reps for that set with your feet elevated, and then build up, just like you did with your Jackknife Pushups.

Eventually, you can build up to the point where your feet are on one chair, and your hands are on two different chairs, so you can lower your chest down between two chairs.

For your Pull-Ups, space your hands wider than shoulder width apart and your palms facing away from you. You should feel an immediate stretch in your lat muscles. Pull up until the base of your neck touches the bar and then lower yourself down.

If you want, you can pull up until the back of your neck touches the bar. Either version will work.

Work up to two sets of six reps, and then up to three sets of eight reps. Flex your lats for six seconds after each set. Your upper body is going to grow very wide, very fast.

Leg Training

At this point, you might be wondering what exercises you should do for your legs. The flexing and tension exercises we discussed earlier for your thighs, hamstrings, and calves will do wonders for your legs. Throw in some running – sprints and mile runs – and your legs are going to look and feel very muscular.

If you're looking for some additional leg work, try doing bodyweight squats, probably the simplest exercise in the world. Stand comfortably with your feet twelve to fifteen inches apart. Look straight ahead and keeping your heels flat on the floor, squat all the way down, and then rise up. You should feel the exercise in your thighs and butt.

Work up to one set of twenty reps, and then progress up to two sets of twenty reps. At that point, you're going to have a choice to make. You can either work up to one set of one hundred reps, or you can do a warm-up set of twenty reps, followed by one or two sets of one-legged squats, probably the most difficult exercise in the world.

To perform a one-legged squat, stand next to a chair or stool and place one hand on it to help you balance. Then raise one leg off the floor, point it straight ahead of you, and attempt to squat down on one leg. Don't be surprised if you fall to the floor.

You can also try this exercise by standing on the seat of a chair – not a chair with wheels on it – placing your hand on the back of the chair, raising one leg, and squatting down. The exercise is actually easier to perform this way as your free leg can point below the level of the chair seat. That change in leverage decreases the resistance you have to push against when you rise.

In either case, proceed with caution. This is a difficult exercise; one that could take you months to master. You might have to work up to quarter reps, then half reps, and only then complete full reps.

Once you are able to complete a full rep, work on completing a set of six reps. Anyone who can complete ten full reps of one-legged squats, all the way down and all the way up, is a monster.

I didn't include any form of squatting in your exercise routine earlier, because leg work can be taxing and most guys who start out in bodybuilding are interested in making fast gains on their chest, shoulders, and arms.

Too much work will cut into your recovery time, so you might want to hold off on squats until after you complete at least one three month cycle on Jackknife Pushups and Chin-Ups.

I've always made my best progress when I performed one core exercise, followed by one assistance exercise, which is what you have with Jackknife Pushups and Chin-Ups. Whenever I started to add on too many exercises, my progress slowed and dried up. Don't make the same mistake.

Extreme Cases

Every now and then I encounter an individual who is so weak they have difficulty just holding the top position in a Jackknife Pushup. Others can barely grip a pull-up bar, and when they do, they can only hold their weight for one second.

Some of these people are cancer patients. Others are simply weak and out of shape. Many were born sickly (as I was), and have had numerous childhood illnesses (as I have). Their conditions were compounded by growing up in a household with abusive parents, parents that fought and bickered, and nothing but junk food to eat (as my household was). If that's the case with you, don't fret. I have the perfect solution.

Perform only the flexing and tension exercises and nothing else. Do them slowly, concentrating on the muscle you are working, and then hold the contraction for a full six seconds.

Do these exercises every day.

Practice flexing various muscles and then try moving your legs and arms, feeling your muscles tense and flex as you move them. You will soon discover some new, unique positions to hold. You'll be inventing your own exercises, which is always cool to do.

You can build a terrific body with nothing more than these flexing and tension exercises. In fact, there's a famous bodybuilder named Maxick who did just that. He was one of the strongest men in the world in his time, and he built his body almost entirely with flexing and tension exercises.

Maxick called his exercise system Muscle Control, and even wrote a book with that same title. You can find it online. It's overpriced at $20 or more, but if you can locate a copy with photographs for under $15, it's definitely worth buying.

Some people claim that Maxick built his body with weights, but they are wrong. He demonstrated his strength with weights; and prior to weightlifting competitions, he trained with weights in order to strengthen his tendons and master the necessary technique involved with each movement. But, as he explains in great detail in his own book with his own words, he built his body with flexing and tension exercises.

Which leads in perfectly to our next chapter.

The Naysayers Will Abound

As your muscles grow and people begin noticing, you're going to be approached by various individuals who will either comment on your physique, or ask you about the program you're following. Common questions include, "What are you doing for your shoulders?", "How did you get your arms so big?", or simply, "How much do you bench?"

Whether you choose to engage these people in conversation is up to you. In my case, if a person approaches me in a sincere way, I always answer their questions and I try to be as helpful as possible. There's a universal brotherhood among bodybuilders, and I do my best to continue that tradition.

If I suspect the questioner is not sincere, I smile and answer them politely, and then move on.

Mixed in among both the sincere and insincere questioners, will be many well-meaning, but confused individuals who, once they learn what kind of program you're following, will tell you that what you're doing is all wrong.

These folks have been brainwashed into believing that the only way to build muscle is with weights. If you tell them you're not using weights, they will react first with disbelief, and then with ridicule. They will also immediately begin to insist that you drop what you're doing and start hitting the weights. Even people with little to no muscle at all will tell you this, which would be laughable if it weren't so sad.

The best way to deal with people like this is to smile and say, "Thanks," and then continue doing what you're doing. Sure, you could engage them in discussion, but you'll find it to be a waste of time. The vast majority of people – upwards of 98% - base their beliefs and their actions on emotions, not facts. Trying to explain to someone who is hooked on weight training why bodyweight training is both safer and more effective is like talking to a wall. Believe me, I've been there and done that.

So remember to smile and thank them, but don't change what you're doing.

As you go through life, you're going to discover that almost everyone you meet forms their belief systems based on emotions, instead of on facts. And that statement is true on any subject, not just bodybuilding.

It's especially true when it comes to politics and religion, with literally hundreds of millions of people around the world adhering to misguided political beliefs and/or following false religions.

There's actually a name for people like this. That name is Useful Idiot.

A useful idiot is someone who supports a belief or ideology, while not truly understanding what that belief or ideology is about, and who is simultaneously held in contempt by the practitioners of that same belief or ideology. In other words, they believe in something that they don't really understand, and are disrespected and looked down upon by the very people they admire, because of their stupidity.

The term "useful idiot" was coined by Vladimar Lenin, the head of Soviet Russia from 1917-22, and the head of the Soviet Union from 1922-24. Lenin invented the term to describe communist sympathizers in the West. While Lenin held these sympathizers in absolute contempt for their stupidity, he realized they were useful tools for spreading propaganda and for helping to brainwash people into accepting and promoting communism.

While Lenin's useful idiots did everything they could to promote communism, the communists themselves went on a mass killing spree, murdering over 100 million people in the 20th century alone. And those 100 million people – the majority of whom were Christians – were only the ones who were murdered. They don't include hundreds of millions more who were beaten, raped, tortured, jailed, or financially ruined. It was the greatest genocide in the history of the world, and it's still continuing today.

There is no better example than communism to illustrate how easily people can be duped and brainwashed. To show you just how crazy this all is, we currently have dozens of politicians in our own country who are self-described communists and socialists. And those same politicians have millions of followers who support and vote for them. Useful idiots, indeed.

Back to bodybuilding: the well-meaning folks who tell you how mistaken you are by not training with weights may not be communists, but they are most certainly useful idiots for promoting a belief they don't truly understand.

Many of them simply won't believe you when you tell them you don't lift weights. In their mind, it's impossible to build huge muscles without weights, and they will project that disbelief onto you. They will think you're lying to them.

If you encounter someone like this, don't get into an argument or a fight; it's just not worth it. Simply shrug and walk away.

Now if you decide to start training with weights at some point, that's up to you. I don't recommend it, but you have the right to do so. I will tell you this: There's nothing that saps your recovery time more than working out with weights.

You can test this out for yourself.

Perform your normal 20 minute workout of Jackknife Push-ups, Chin-Ups, and flexing exercises. Note how you feel afterwards, and note how you feel an hour or two later. In most cases, you will be 80-90% recovered within a couple of hours.

Now rest a day or two and then perform a 20 minute workout with weights. Note how you feel afterwards, and note how you feel an hour or two later. In most cases, you will feel tired and sluggish. You might even want to take a nap. That's the effect the weights have on your recovery ability.

Training with weights will drain your energy in other ways, as well. When you are forced to balance an external weight – such as a weighted barbell or weighted dumbbells – it produces a strain throughout your entire central nervous system. That's debilitating.

Compound that with multiple sets done over multiple workouts and you're looking at a recipe for disaster.

There's a machine called a posturometer. It's a meter that measures posture, and it uses a numerical system to show how much tilt and rotation a person has in their spine. A rating of 7 or higher is considered extremely out of alignment. No one with a rating that high should be lifting anything heavy.

Now get this: Almost everyone who trains with weights has a posturometer rating of 10 or higher. In other words, their spines are severely out of alignment. Does that sound like fun to you?

You might be familiar with the name John Madden. He's an ex-NFL head coach. In fact, he won a Super Bowl as the head coach of the Oakland Raiders. After he retired from coaching, Madden became a television broadcaster and regularly appeared on Monday Night Football.

One night, Madden made a very revealing comment. A player had just been injured and was being carted off the field. Madden's fellow broadcaster mentioned how muscular the player was and how he was always in the gym lifting weights.

Madden nodded and said that players who spend the most time working out with weights were always the first ones to get injured.

Martial artists have told me the same thing.

So think before you leap.

Consider the consequences if you do decide to start training with weights.

You can build a magnificent body without weights. You can do it fast and in complete safety.

You can build a magnificent body with weights. It will take you longer and your body will be at risk of injury. Eventually, your spine will go out of alignment.

In the first case (training without weights), you will finish your workouts feeling energized and full of life.

In the second case (training with weights), you will finish your workouts with various degrees of fatigue. Eventually, you will begin to feel rundown and lethargic.

You might even injure yourself, either while working out, or while participating in sports or some other activity.

Which approach sounds better to you?

No one ever injured themselves, or threw their spine out of alignment, by doing Jackknife Pushups or Chin-Ups. No one ever hurt themselves doing a Pushup on the floor. However, millions of people have injured themselves, and millions more have thrown their spines out of alignment, while lifting weights.

Put that in your pipe and smoke it.

Plug Those Energy Leaks!

Earlier, we spoke of the importance of sleep and rest. Along with that, there's also emotional stress. Emotional stress will sap both your energy and your recovery time. You won't make a lot of bodybuilding progress if you're under emotional stress, so let's talk about how to deal with it.

Let's start with parents.

If your parents don't understand you, don't let it get you down. The truth is most parents don't have a clue what their kids are going through. They're so stressed out trying to make a living, while simultaneously dealing with a world gone seemingly mad that their minds are preoccupied.

It's nothing against you personally; they're just stressed to the max. So cut your parents a little slack.

It won't be long before you've moved out on your own and then there will be plenty of moments when you wish you were back at home, letting someone else deal with the bills and problems. You may scoff at this now, but believe me, almost everyone I know has experienced it. You will, too.

Have you ever heard the expression Silence Is Golden?

Well, if you find yourself unable to talk with your parents without arguing, then it might be a good idea not to talk to them at all. At least for the time being. It's better to hold your tongue now, rather than to say something you end up regretting later.

If your parents are either unwilling or unable to supply you with the healthy, muscle-building foods you want, you're just going to have to raise the money and buy them yourself. That's what I did.

While other kids my age were playing sports, going on dates, and having fun, I was working. Always working. I had no social life and no fun at all growing up. It was a lousy tradeoff, but I wanted muscles and health, and I was willing to do whatever it took to get them. Most likely, you won't have to go to that extreme.

If you're lucky enough to have parents that are understanding and helpful, that's fantastic. If not, that's fantastic too. Make up your mind that you will succeed in whatever you set out to do, whether you have their backing, or whether you have to do it entirely on your own.

Next up is school and government bureaucracy, and you can throw society in there, as well. I'm going to tell you something now that very few people know, and that no one else in your entire life is likely to tell you. Are you ready? Here it is: Almost everything you learned in school outside of math, science, and English; almost everything your parents have ever told you about history and life; almost everything you've seen on television, on the internet, on a movie screen, or read in the newspaper, is a big, fat, bold-faced lie.

Now I'm not saying your teachers and your parents lied to you on purpose. What I'm saying is the information they gave you was wrong. It wasn't necessarily their fault; most likely, they repeated the same lies that they were taught and believed to be true.

Some of this you may have already sensed on your own. If you've ever dealt with an ignorant teacher or school official; if you're ever encountered a rule, a law, or something in life that didn't make sense at all, then you have an inkling of what I'm talking about.

If you want to know the truth about life, the truth about history, the truth about how the world works, you're going to have to do a lot of reading and studying on your own. And it's going to be a lifelong process, because with every lie you uncover, you're going to discover many more lies. Like the Hydra in mythology – a creature that sprouted two heads every time one head was cut off – every lie you encounter in life will lead to more lies.

If that's not bad enough, media and internet censorship is making it more and more difficult to discern truth from fiction. Websites and videos that attempt to honestly address political and social issues are being shut down, while those that propagate lies are left to flourish.

Even worse, at this very moment, laws are being passed in this country in order to silence people from speaking honestly. It's actually becoming illegal to tell the truth.

All of this is extremely stressful and you will need to guard yourself from becoming depressed over it. If you want to know the truth about any particular subject, you can always email me and I'll do my best to give you an honest answer. Outside of that, you're going to have your work cut out for you.

Here's another shocker for you: most people are complete ignoramuses. Obviously, you're not, or you wouldn't be reading this book. But most people – the vast majority of people on earth – certainly are. And dealing with ignoramuses every day of your life is also stressful. Especially when they're people you care about.

That's why friends can be a source of emotional stress. As you grow, both physically and mentally, you'll notice many people around you stagnating and going nowhere. In many cases, they'll be confused by and/or jealous of the changes they observe in you. Some will desert you. Others will fall silently by the wayside. You'll meet new friends along the way, of course, but still your journey will be lonely at times. That's where the expression It's Lonely at the Top comes from.

And that leads us to girls. Contrary to what you may think, or what your buddies might be telling you, girls are not the be-all and end-all of your existence. In fact, you would do well to remember that throughout history more men have been ruined and destroyed by women, than for all other reasons combined.

As your muscles grow, and as you mature, grow as a person, and expand your mind, girls will become attracted to you. That's all well and good, but the moment you start thinking that your life is over, because some girl doesn't like you, or because you can't seem to generate interest in any girl at all, you're doomed.

As a man, your primary focus should be on honoring God. After that, it should be on working, creating, and building. That's your job, so to speak. You're here to be a father and a provider to your family. You're here to be a creator. You're here to protect and care for women and children, when the need arises. In other words, you're here to be a man.

Modern society has this all turned upside down. They don't want you to be a man. Laws are being passed right now as I type this that are designed to strip away your manhood and turn you into a guilt-ridden, soy-boy leftist. Don't let them do it to you.

Society wants you to be a consumer. But that's not who you are. Men are builders and achievers, not consumers. Your life does not revolve around the latest iPhone, the newest car, the coolest video game, the hippest fashion, or anything at all that emanates from the cesspool known as Hollywood.

Women and soy-boys are consumers, not you. Let them obsess over the latest gadgets and toys.

You're a man.

You're here to honor God, and to perform meaningful work. Everything good and noble and useful in the world was created by men, just like you.

Every great battle of history was fought by men, just like you.

Every instance of good triumphing over evil was achieved by men, just like you.

Know who you are. And then act accordingly.

Don't fall for the myth of romantic love: the ridiculous idea that one day you will meet the perfect girl and from that point on, life will be wonderful. Nothing could be further from the truth.

The idea of romantic love was conjured up approximately three hundred years ago. It was created by individuals with way too much time on their hands and with very little experience in male/female relationships. Over the last 70-80 years, the idea of romantic love has been pushed and popularized by songs, movies, and television.

The reality is romantic love does not exist. For thousands of years, young men and young women married at the age of thirteen or fourteen. Then they raised a family together.

Chances are, if you are currently in middle school or high school, then if you had been born in an earlier generation, you'd be married right now and living with a girl your own age that your parents and grandparents picked out for you. Take a look at the girls in your school. If you had been born 500 years ago, you'd be married to one of them right now. How do you like them apples?

When people married in earlier generations, it had nothing to do with romantic love. Their husbands and their wives were picked by their parents and other relatives. The bride and groom had little or no choice in the matter. It's called an arranged marriage. And you want to know something? They worked. Divorce was almost non-existent. Families were stable. Societies were stable. That's all gone now.

Don't waste time and energy pursuing romantic love. Pursue female companionship, if you want. But don't be misled into believing that one day you are going to meet the perfect girl, or that you need a girl to make your life complete.

You want a companion that's pretty, obviously. But personality far outshines looks. You want a girl that believes in you and supports you. Someone that makes you feel important. Someone who understands that a man is the head of the household. Don't get involved with anyone who doesn't believe that.

Don't get involved with any girl who wouldn't fit into your long range plans of marriage. All you'll be doing is wasting both her time and your time.

Don't get involved with any girl who says she's a feminist.

Don't get involved with any girl who fawns over celebrities.

Don't get involved with any girl who isn't pro-life.

Leave the feminists, and the celebrity chasers, and the pro-aborts to the soy-boys. They need love too.

Now if you meet a girl who says she's a feminist, but she doesn't really understand what a feminist is, or is unaware of feminism's communist origins (feminism was created by the Communist Party in order to subjugate and enslave women, while simultaneously destroying the family unit); someone who's been duped, but who is willing listen to reason, someone whom you might be able to change, that's different. You might be able to get somewhere with her. You might actually be able to sustain a relationship with her and turn her into a sensible human being. That's certainly possible, but the odds are stacked against you.

As you go through life, girls will be attracted to you.

If you want their companionship, don't chase them. Let them come to you.

The easiest and best way to go about this is to spend your time honoring God, and performing meaningful and uplifting work. Be the best student you can. Be the best athlete that you can. Be the best creator that you can. Be the best man that you can. You will not have any difficulty attracting girls.

Don't be afraid to say, "Hi" to a girl you like, or to initiate a conversation. Just keep it casual.

Smile. Be friendly. Use appropriate humor. Learn their name and use it (people like when others use their name).

Act like a man when you're with a girl. In other words, don't do anything stupid. Don't act immature. Use proper etiquette. Open the door for her. If you're with her on the sidewalk, walk on the outside, closest to the street. If you're on a bus, train, or plane, sit on the outside, closest to the aisle.

Avoid elaborate dates; they're a waste of time and money. Do things that are free and casual, such as a walk at the park or beach, a visit to a free museum, or any place where you can sit and talk.

Carnivals are cheap and fun places to take or meet a girl.

Parties are okay, but be prepared to deal with drunks and jackasses.

School activities are okay. They're usually free.

Forget concerts. They're expensive and the music stinks. A concert of classical music is an exception, but you probably won't find a girl who's into classical music. If you do, you're a lucky man.

If you really want to impress a girl, take some classes in public speaking and join the debate team at your school. Then, when your presentation is polished, invite her to one of your debates.

Nothing strikes more fear in adults than public speaking. And nothing demonstrates strength, courage, and confidence better than a smooth public speaker.

Public speaking is also one of the rarest and most sought-after skills in existence. It will brand you a winner and contribute immensely to the quality of your life.

Don't brag about your dates, or about what happened, or what didn't happen on your dates to your buddies. You're better off keeping all that stuff to yourself.

Don't fool around outside of marriage. Yes, I'm serious. I'll tell you why in the last chapter.

We've discussed a number of factors here that contribute to emotional stress. Don't let any of them disturb your equilibrium. Stay poised and in control at all times.

Remember, you're a man.

Bodybuilding as Self-Defense

I've never known anyone – other than myself – who has made the connection between bodybuilding and self-defense. But to me that connection is obvious: bodybuilding is a deterrent to assault.

To better understand this, consider that predators, both human and animal, share a common trait: They pick on the weak.

Makes sense, doesn't it? After all, why should a predator risk injury or even death by attacking a strong opponent - someone who is likely to fight back and capable of injuring them - when they could just as easily single out an opponent that is weak and unlikely to offer any meaningful resistance?

If you're being bullied or picked on at school, then bodybuilding is one of the best things you could possibly do. Because once those muscles of yours start to sprout up, you'll be pleasantly surprised to learn that those same bullies will start leaving you alone. They'll look for someone smaller and weaker to pick on.

Now there are some people who are so desperate and so stupid they'll attack the strong, as well as the weak. But those cases are rare. Most predators will leave a strong person alone.

Still, it's a good idea to pay a visit to your local boxing club and ask for a couple of lessons. You don't have to spend months working on the speed bag or sparring in the ring. Just tell the instructor you want to learn how to throw some punches and combinations for self-defense in a street fight. He'll know what to show you, so pay attention. And then practice what he teaches you. Hopefully, you'll never have to use it.

You may also want to take a few wrestling, grappling, or aikido lessons. Aikido focuses on joint locks and throws. The locks come in handy when you're grappling with an opponent.

Be ready to defend yourself, if necessary, but never start a fight or give someone else a reason to attack you. For one thing, you never know who you're messing with. If you pick a fight with someone and it turns out they're a trained MMA fighter, you're in trouble. If they have a gun, it's even worse. You could lose your life over some silly little disagreement.

So mind your own business. Most people will leave you alone if you treat them with respect, which often means keeping your mouth shut.

There are also legal ramifications when it comes to violence. Not too long ago, if somebody insulted you, or your mother, or your girlfriend, and you punched that person in the nose, the cops would look the other way. They figured the guy had it coming to him based on what he said. Those days are over.

Today you can get arrested for fighting no matter what the cause or who started it. You can even get arrested for defending yourself from robbery and attempted murder. In places like London, Sweden, Germany, and South Africa, if an armed criminal – or a gang of armed criminals – breaks into your home late at night, while you and your children are asleep, and you kill one of them in self-defense, you will likely be arrested and charged with murder. I'm not kidding.

You can get arrested even if their intent was to murder you and your children, and you injured one of them in self-defense. That's how twisted things have become.

And it's only getting worse. In those same countries, and many other countries, you can get arrested simply for telling the truth. Yes, I'm serious. The truth is outlawed in many places throughout the world. And it's quickly becoming that way in the United States.

You might have heard the terms "political correctness" and "hate speech." Political correctness is nothing more than a means of making it socially unacceptable to tell the truth. Hate speech is nothing more than telling the truth.

Political correctness has run amok in the United States, and laws are now being passed in this country, which make it illegal to tell the truth.

The end game is control, and outlawing self-defense is part of that control. If leftist politicians had their way, all guns would be outlawed and self-defense in any form would be illegal. That's literally what they're striving for.

As I type these very words, a Dallas County District Attorney announced that he will no longer prosecute people who steal personal items worth $750 or less. Once again, I'm not kidding. You don't have to be a rocket scientist to see where this is going.

If someone breaks into your house and steals your brand new suit, or your shoes, or your television, it's not a crime, according to this district attorney. His office will determine that the person who stole from you was poor and couldn't afford a new suit, or new shoes, or a new television, so all criminal charges against them will be dropped. Even worse, if you arrive home when the theft is occurring and use force to protect your property, *you* will be arrested and charged with a crime.

If someone robs you in a supermarket parking lot and steals all the food you just bought for you and your family, this district attorney's office will say that the person who stole from you was hungry and couldn't afford to feed themselves, so no crime was committed. But if you fight with that person and try to prevent them from stealing from you, well, the same district attorney's office will charge you with assault.

In the city of Seattle, similar action is occurring. Just last week, a man who had been convicted of assault and rape was freed from prison after only nine months, because the judicial system in that city felt his punishment was too harsh. What do you think happened next?

The man in question immediately returned to the scene of his previous crime and assaulted the same woman he had previously raped. And then he took off. He's on the loose right now, free as a bird.

How would you feel if that woman he raped and assaulted was your sister, or your mother, or your girlfriend, or your wife?

It's a crazy world we live in. So be careful out there.

Lock your doors, both at home and in your car.

Don't leave anything visible lying on your car seat.

Don't flaunt your money or brag about how much money you have. In fact, be careful when taking money out of your pocket. You don't want anyone seeing how much money you're carrying. It might give them ideas.

You may have heard the expression, "An ounce of prevention is worth a pound of cure." There's a lot of truth to that statement.

You can prevent trouble from starting by practicing situational awareness when you're out in public.

Situational awareness means being aware of what's happening around you at all times.

Never let a person you don't know get behind you. If one does, calmly turn to the side and keep them in your peripheral vision. If their intent was to harm you, they'll know that they've now lost the element of surprise.

I can't tell you how many times the simple act of being aware has prevented someone from attempting to rob or attack me. In one instance, it may have saved my life when some punk tried pulling the "knockout game" on me. Out of the corner of my eye, I saw him coming at me with his fist up ready to strike and I was able to respond accordingly.

Another time, a punk followed me and then hid behind the side of a vending machine that I stopped to use. He was waiting for me to pull money out of my pocket with the intent to rob me.

Because I knew he was there, I braced myself. I was ready to slam his head into the vending machine as soon as he made his move.

He could tell I was aware of his presence and he chickened out. That was an attempted robbery thwarted, thanks to situational awareness.

Those are just two of the many examples I could list for you. In most cases, being aware will prevent an attack from occurring. In the rare case where an attack does occur, being aware will leave you ready to respond.

Some things are worth fighting for, such as defending yourself or your family. Other things aren't, like an insult from some punk you don't know and will probably never see again. Learn to understand the difference.

Be aware of your surroundings at all times.

Never relax.

Saving Your Soul - Your Ultimate Challenge

We've talked of many things, you and I, and now we come to the most important chapter in this entire book.

Follow the guidelines in this book faithfully and very soon you will have a strong and muscular body; a body that others admire. Best of all, you'll admire yourself. You'll have more confidence, you'll look better, and you'll feel better. Bodybuilding not only improves your body, it improves every other aspect of your life.

That's all great news, but when you really get down to it, your body, your muscles, and your physical appearance have no bearing at all on your ultimate life goal, which is to get to Heaven.

I've been straight with you throughout this entire book, and I'm going to be straight with you now: There's one way, and only one way, to get to Heaven, and that's to accept, embrace, and practice the true Catholic faith. Because without the true Catholic faith, the faith that Jesus Christ Himself handed down to us, you ain't getting there.

If that bothers you, I'm sorry, but the truth is the truth.

As Saint Thomas Aquinas said, "The greatest charity one can do to another is to lead him to the truth."

Want proof that the true Catholic faith is the only way to get to Heaven? Read the book *Outside the Catholic Church There is Absolutely No Salvation* by Brother Peter Dimond. You can find it online at www.MostHolyFamilyMonastery.com.

If you can't afford to buy the book, which sells for around twenty bucks, then visit the website and read all of the free information. Watch the free videos. Immerse yourself in the truth. One thing's for sure, you won't be able to dispute anything in the book or on the website. I absolute guarantee it.

Now when I say the true Catholic faith, I mean just that: the true Catholic faith, which is the faith that existed publicly up until the 1960s, and still exists today in small pockets. What you see coming out of Rome today is not the true Catholic faith. What you see today coming out of the schools and churches that call themselves Catholic is not the true Catholic faith. They represent a counterfeit church, not the true Catholic Church.

A lot of people get confused by that. They see what's been happening for the last 60 years, with a succession of counterfeit Anti-Popes, counterfeit Cardinals and Bishops, and counterfeit priests that have not been validly ordained, and they say, "Wait a second. How can all this corruption, all this scandal, all this evil that I see coming from the Catholic Church represent the true church of Jesus Christ?"

The answer is they don't represent the true church of Jesus Christ, because they are not part of the true Catholic Church. They represent a counterfeit church. The true Catholic Church was infiltrated and subverted by Communists almost a century ago.

Have you ever seen a counterfeit twenty dollar bill? At first glance, it looks just like the real thing. However, when you take a closer look, it's clear that the bill is phony. And when you take a real close look, the fakery is so obvious that you wonder how you were ever fooled in the first place.

The same thing happens when you take a close look at the counterfeit church that's pretending to be Catholic. The fakery becomes so obvious that you wonder how anyone could be so easily duped.

In order to see the truth, however, it's necessary to leave emotions out of the equation and apply facts, logic, and evidence. Sadly, most people are not able to do that.

Remember what we spoke about earlier, about how people make their decisions and justify their actions based on emotions, rather than facts? Well, this is a big one here. The deception of the counterfeit church is so huge, so monstrous, and so evil that hundreds of millions of people simply refuse to acknowledge it.

These folks are so frightened of the truth that the majority of them refuse to even look at the evidence. They won't read the book I mentioned above, or visit the website of the publisher. In fact, just mentioning this subject causes their hands to shake and the spittle to fly from their mouths.

The real question is, how will you react?

Do you have the courage to read *Outside the Catholic Church There Is Absolutely No Salvation*?

Are you brave enough to visit the publisher's website and research the issue for yourself?

If your answer is yes, then I applaud you.

If your answer is no, then I challenge you to summon your courage and prove me wrong by refuting the information in the book and on the website.

You won't be able to do it, but I challenge you anyway, because in your search to prove the truth wrong, you just might awaken to the truth.

Now if you're really courageous; if you're the absolute bravest of the brave, the strongest of the strong; afraid of no man and willing to do whatever it takes to achieve eternal glory, then read the book *Preparation for Death* by Saint Alphonsus Liguori.

I must warn you, it's not for the squeamish. You'll need the strength of Sampson to even begin reading it, and most men are too cowardly and too weak to do that.

Sadly, it's that same cowardice and that same weakness and inability to resist sin that causes the vast majority of men and women to be condemned to an eternity burning in the fires of hell.

What about you?

Where do you stand?

You want muscles? You got 'em. Just follow the directions in this book.

You want to get to Heaven? You got that too. Just follow the true Catholic faith.

God doesn't fool around. You either get with His program, or you spend eternity burning in the fires of hell.

The choice is yours.

As always, you can email me with any questions you have.

THE END ... of this book – and the beginning of a new life ... for you.

THANK YOU VERY MUCH for buying this book. If you enjoyed it, please share your thoughts by posting a review on Amazon or wherever you purchased the book. People often make their book-reading decisions based on other people's reviews (I know I do), and your review of this book could be the deciding factor for someone who is wondering whether or not to read it. Even a short, one sentence review will help. Thank you again.

The North Hollywood Detective Club Series

THE CASE OF THE HOLLYWOOD ART HEIST

Jeffrey Jones is a kid with a problem. A *lot* of problems. He's laughed at in school. The neighborhood bully has it out for him. And his parents treat him like a six-year-old. However, Jeffrey does have one ace up his sleeve: He's a master investigator.

When the brother of a friend is arrested for stealing a valuable painting, Jeffrey and his best friend, Pablo Reyes, form The North Hollywood Detective Club and set out to rescue him from jail. Their investigation leads them to a mysterious tattoo parlor, a glamorous television star, and a 20-year-old unsolved murder.

THE CASE OF THE DEAD MAN'S TREASURE

A treasure worth killing for. Hired by their teacher to find the driver responsible for a hit-and-run car accident, Jeffrey Jones and Pablo Reyes stumble upon a search for an ancient treasure and a ruthless treasure hunter who will stop at nothing to get his hands on the prize.

THE CASE OF THE CHRISTMAS COUNTERFEITERS

Two teen detectives. One criminal mastermind. And two billion dollars in counterfeit currency. What could possibly go wrong?

While the rest of the world prepares to celebrate Christmas, teen super sleuths Jeffrey Jones and Pablo Reyes uncover a plot to flood the city of Los Angeles with billions of dollars in counterfeit currency. Their investigation leads them to a master criminal, his hoodlum son, and a mysterious 15-year-old girl, who holds the key to the entire puzzle.

THE CASE OF THE DEADLY DOUBLE-CROSS

Teen detectives Jeffrey Jones and Pablo Reyes are hired by an older classmate to find her missing father. But when the man turns up dead, they're framed for his murder. On the run from the law, and with only their friends Marisol and Susie to help them, the boys engage in a frantic search to catch the real killer, before the police catch them.

Other Books by Mike Mains

MONKEY JOKES – A JOKE BOOK FOR KIDS!

Kids love monkeys and they're guaranteed to go bananas over the world's first and funniest collection of monkey jokes. Are you ready for a gorillian laughs? Then stop monkeying around and get this book today!

Mike Mains writes mystery and adventure books for sleuths of all ages. He can be reached at mainsmike@yahoo.com

Made in the USA
Monee, IL
26 February 2023

28764949R00039